Deepstep
Come
Shining

C.D. Wright

DEEPSTEP COME SHINING

C.D. Wright

COPPER CANYON PRESS
Port Townsend, Washington

ALSO BY C.D. WRIGHT:

Alla Breve Loving
Room Rented by a Single Woman
Terrorism
Translations of the Gospel Back into Tongues
Further Adventures with You
String Light
Just Whistle, with photographs by Deborah Luster
The Lost Roads Project: A Walk-in Book of Arkansas, with photographs
    by Deborah Luster
The Reader's Map of Arkansas
Tremble

A chapbook from *Deepstep Come Shining* was published in *Black Warrior Review* (Vol. 24, No. 2). Additional passages from the poem were previously published in *Fence.* The author gratefully acknowledges the editors for printing these excerpts.

Copper Canyon Press would like to thank Deborah Luster for the use of *Rosesucker Retablo, III.*

The publication of this book was supported by grants from the Lannan Foundation, the National Endowment for the Arts, and the Washington State Arts Commission. Additional support was received from Elliott Bay Book Company, Cynthia Hartwig, and the many members who joined the Friends of Copper Canyon Press campaign. Copper Canyon Press is in residence with Centrum at Fort Worden State Park.

LIBRARY OF CONGRESS CATALOGING-IN-PUBLICATION DATA
Wright, C.D., 1949–
Deepstep come shining / by C.D. Wright.
   p. cm.
ISBN 1-55659-093-8
ISBN 1-55659-092-X (pbk.)
1. Southern States – Poetry. I. Title.
PS3573.R497 D22 1998
811'.54 – DDC21   98-40084
                        CIP

9 8 7 6 5 4 3 2 FIRST EDITION

COPPER CANYON PRESS
Post Office Box 271
Port Townsend, Washington 98368

for Alyce Collins Wright
Court Reporter for 11th Chancery District of Arkansas
1961–1975

for Fern Raulston Nicholson
Court Reporter for 14th Judicial Circuit of Arkansas
1951–1990

Deepstep
Come
Shining

C.D. Wright

LEAR: *... you see how this world goes.*
GLOUCESTER: *I see it feelingly.*

Lead me, guide me to the light of your paper. Keep me in your arc of acuity. And when the ream is spent. Write a poem on my back. I'll never wash it off.

Meanwhile the cars continued in a persistent flow down
Closeburn Road.

The refrain to the rain would be a movement up and down the
clefs of light.

Chlorophyll world. July. Great goblets of magnolialight.

Her head cooling against the car glass. The mind apprehends
the white piano, her mother. Who played only what she chose,
who chose only to play "Smoke Gets in Your Eyes."

A stadium emptied. The ruby progression of taillights. The
eyes' ability to perceive a series of still images as continuous
motion. Time lapse.

This wasn't movie traffic. There weren't twenty people to
see *Smoke.*

At the drive-in. When they were young. The parents were
young. The children falling asleep on the hood with the motor
warm. Coating the ornamental swan with their prints. The
projectionist's private life: shadows animating a wall.

"Never avert your eyes." (Kurosawa)

A photograph is a writing of the light. *Photo Graphein.*

More than magnolia, crepe myrtle is missed. The white bushes especially.

Against undifferentiated dark. It is unlike night.

She will still be up when we come in. Our floating host. She will be at the door in her pleated nightgown. Admit us into her air-conditioned nightgown. Her glory cloud.

In the seclusionary cool of the car the mind furnishes a high-ceilinged room with a white piano. Seldom struck. Color sensations. In which the piano floats on a black marble lake, mute swan in a dark room. Beyond the windshield the land claims saturate levels of green. Illuminating figures and objects. Astonishing our earthliness. I was there. I know.

Everyone in their car needs love. Car love. Meat love. Money love. Pass with care.

Deepstep, Baby. Deepstep.

The boneman said he would take the blinded to the river. With a mirror. And then what.

The boneman said he would take the blinded into a darkened room. And put a hot-herb poultice on their sightless face.

Mullein for this mullein for that. We called it flannel.

Then leave them there.

The baby sister of the color photographer had a baby girl in the hills. Born with scooped-out sockets in the head. Born near the tracks they sprayed with Agent Orange. The railroad's denials, ditto the army's.

They would have been blue. The eyes. She did not have. Blue as the chicory in yonder ditch.

We see a little farther now and a little farther still

She said her lights would be on and they were

Groping around the sleeping house in our gowns

Peeping into the unseen

Beautiful things fill every vacancy

Ripcord Lounge is up on the right. 32° beer. A little past the
package store. Suddenly I have the feeling of a great victory.
A delirious brilliance.

All around in here it used to be so pretty.

The boneman's bobcat. Its untamable eyes in the night. Did you
know a ghost has hair. A ghost has hair. That's right.

Peaches and fireworks and red ants.
Now do you know where you are.

I boarded with a suitcase of Blackbeard fireworks. I had
forgotten about the Unabomber. They shook me down.
Confiscated my sparklers, my Roman candles, my ladyfingers.

Make a left just beyond Pulltight Road.

The land obtained in exchange for two blind horses. This land
became known as Wrens.

Merely listening

After the rain the trees smell so pleased

The hale sleep naked atop the sheets

We leave the deck for the lawn

The grasses licking our feet

A semicircle of chairs opens a parenthesis

In the direction of the lightsource

We see a little farther now and a little farther still

Peeping into the unseen

Why is she so kind. Our floating host. Why am I so stingy
and vain.

A baseball diamond in every hamlet.

The waitresses in hairnets. Nurse-caps. Employees must pluck
out an eye before returning to work.

Cold eyes are bad to eat.

You lied. She doesn't have air-conditioning. She is long in bed. Note on the fridge: Vanilla yogurt inside. See you in the morning, girls. How did you like *Smoke.* No one should know the hour or the day.

We will become godlike.

Open the window. That the glory cloud may come and go.

Inside the iris of time, the iridescent dreaming kicks in. Turn off that stupid damn machine.

Kepler's invention of the *camera lucida* fell into oblivion some two hundred years. There is no avoiding oblivion.

Where does this damn stupid thing go. For god's sake. Are you sure you want to wear that.

Especially in this one-stoplight town. Watch out for "the swerve of smalltown eyes." (Agee) Feel them trained on you in unison.

Boiled peanuts. Now that *is* an acquired taste.

Once the eye is enucleated. Would you replace it with wood, ivory, bone, shell, or a precious stone. Who invented the glass eye. Guess. The Venetians. Of course.

Go to Venice; bring me back a mason jar of glass eyes. They shall multiply like shadflies.

The antinomian marsupial in the road fixing us in her eyeshine, *tapeta lucida.* The objective is hopeless – abandon the baseball diamond for the strip mall. Nothing arboreal to correct the view. The Dumpster behind Long John Silver's berths the opossum in its postnuptial fast-food armor. Slower now, go slow. SPEED   HECKED BY RADAR. O lucky stars. Motel 6 left its light on for us. Remember you are nothing without credit.

In Rome (likewise-built-on-seven-hills), Georgia, the citizens hail their fellows as Romans. We never found the Forum. The arrows continued pointing right. And a sculpture of Remus and Romulus. Given by Il Duce to the Romans of Georgia. Stored in a root cellar during the war.

It follows that in Athens, Georgia, the citizens hail their fellows as Athenians.

West of Rome is Poetry. Poetry, Georgia. Wonder who lives there.

In the antique store, voices emanating from the pots.

How I miss the white piano. Only in the fovea. Where the photoreceptors are so concentrated. Maximal sight.

Keep me in your arc of acuity. *Siempre, por favor.*

Maybe you should turn the air conditioner off. We're not moving. The rain gives but brief relief.

I'd take the boneman over the snakeman, but when the snakeman talked about walking his six-point stag home through the pecan orchard, I felt a twinge of envy for the gentle living that can go on in the country. And when I peer inside the cage the boneman keeps the bobcat in, I feel a twinge of ill will toward his ignorance.

Deepstep. People just know what they know. (Come shining.)

The chicken's name is Becky. They found her a good home with a peahen for fellowship. Chicken love.

Don't park in the shade on my account.

If we let the windows down we can hear Cape Fear. Exhaust stink. Or is that Hog Waste Lagoon. Man alive, that's foul.

Get your bearings. Hear the trees.

The silver threads of Spanish moss dripping from the telephone wires. It flies here. In pianolight. Like ghost hair.

```
                E   R         S
T P H
T   H A     E           S
    P   A         R     TS
    K
    P H A           B G
      W     O       PB
      H     O O           L
            O           R
TK          E           T
      H R   EU
            EU      L
              F P L T
T P                     T
S   W A           P L
                  P
TW    R
    P       E   PB
S               EU    L   S
            A
S           E   R
            EU          S
              F
        RA          PB
TK      O       P L
T P H       U   P L   S
            O
S           O
    PW    O           PB   S
              U
    K       O
    W       EU  PB
    K   A       R B
        O       R
        A
    K       O       PB
S       R   E   R       T
            EU  BL
              F P L T
T P         U R
TKPW        EUF
            E   PB
T P H A         P L   S
    P       E   PB
S           EU      L   D
            O
            A
ST      R   EU  PB  G
              F
        R   EU  B   S
              F P L T
        W A     FR    T
S   W A         P L
                P
TK    R
S       A               S
              F P L T
    K       O       P L
    P HR   EU
              F P L T
```

Healers in these parts can make one WHOLE or deathly ill.
If the swamp doctor pencils a series of random numbers on
some bones you could win cash or a convertible. If your given
name is penciled on a string of ribs. Whatever the swamp
doctor says. Comply. Whether a believer or not. Remember
Pascal shewed our very air has weight. It can be measured.

Writ by hand. Crudely executed. In the hopeless objective of
receiving the marvels that come to one by sight, sound, and
touch, merely in order:

To feather
To cream
To fall to the knees
To chicory
To fold
To coax (a tomato)
To keep a pet (antelope)
To rain but brief relief
To river
To shield
To watch
To fiddle (rain or shine)
To ride. To eat.
To have black hair.
To see to feel WHOLES
To stick out
To poke around
To spit
To bleach
To suddenly
To know the Veals (of Deepstep)
To sleep (hale)
To continue (in a persistent flow

It's the year of the magicicadae. Seventeen years underground. Boring slowly upward. Ever so slowly. To get to the surface in the spring of the seventeenth year, it will scrabble through pavement. With not a minute to spare except for sex and song.

It must escape its carapace. Quickly. We must all escape our carapace. Come shining.

The day animals need to be able to distinguish colors. And the night creatures must manage low levels of light.

The white piano *is* her mother. And it fills with petals. Ghost hair. Who shot the piano. Killed the mother. And made the daughter to suffer.

The cat has guanine in the retina. Extra sensitive. In Yeats's version Oscar Wilde's father enucleates his patient's eye at the dining-room table and the cat eats it. "Cats love eyes," the cat lover reassures his patient.

Onionlight. Vidalia onions. That's right. Now do you know where you are.

The boneman said apply flax and whites of eggs to bleeding eyes.

So Gloucester had to smell his way to Dover.

But we aren't going there. Or anywhere the air does not smell of barbecue.

The preacher considers Whitey's Drive-In his parish.

What did you buy at the 20-cent table.

Where do you folks live at. Between the *a* and the *t*.

Take a mirror to the river. Then what. The young woman shuffles into the boneman's shed, and he brings her a jar of fermented swamp mulch from the closet. To make the swelling go down. Leglight.

First visual memory: one of vagrant white splotches in a clearing, a fat, diapered baby in a field of timothy chasing another diapered bottom through the timothy. Last visual memory: one of vagrant white splotches in a clearing, a fat, diapered baby in a field of timothy chasing another diapered bottom through the timothy. When it's mowed, and the fodder's fresh. I remember. I was there. No other features vex the view. Not the barn, the Gold Bond Medicated Powder sign fading from its highway plane. The black dog tearing after us. (*Night,* the black lab, the family's ecstatic.) The specific lighting from the sky never impinged upon the eye. Not individualized rocks. Split-rail fencing edged with fleabane. The proximity of a neglected pitchfork. Never never never...

Alligator couple bowed up and trolling the swamp alongside.
Can they reach the shore before we can reach the car door.
Watching them watching us plan our getaway.

This is where Michael Jordan's father napped in his Lexus.
Near Lumberton where Shelby's darling was born. Lexus love.

Everyone in their convertible needs love.

So what did you think of the movie *Smoke*.

I liked the business about Bakhtin rotting in prison, fresh out of
rolling papers. Smoking his manuscript.

Morning glories. What's your favorite.

Pull in at Chuck's Dollar Store I want to buy some Visine, some
X-acto blades.

The land obtained in exchange for two blind horses. This land
became known as Wrens.

If you bought that bobcat you could set it free. Then you would
need to go back and turn the dogs loose. They're just as
miserable. Pet one pet the other. And the chickens on top of
each other in the miniature coop in the Red Flyer. One of those
chickens could be Becky's kin. Chicken love.

Since he left my Red Flyer out for trash pickup I've been shouldering one rock at a time. Never throw out any thing whatsoever on wheels.

He was here; then he was gone. He came for his money. Name of Broomhead. I said, O go on.

Love it Leave it Love it Leave it Love it Love it Leave it Love it

And we all shine on.

The boneman hung up a sheet, slashed it, and ordered the blinded one stick his arm through, then he stuck thorns in their sightless arm.

There are enough signs. Of the lack of tenderness in the world. And yet. And yet. All you have to do is ask. Anyone here can extol the virtues of an onion. Where to get barbecue minced, pulled, or chopped. The hour of the day they have known the thorn of love.

I'm a little bit queasy about the boneman's acupuncture.

There may be an ordinance against clotheslines. In Shelby's old neighborhood, there was an ordinance against walking on certain streets with a lunch bucket. And on and on and on.

The sky, convict grey.

I didn't like the snakeman. He had a shitty attitude.

And if thy right eye offend thee pluck it out.

Love it Leave it Love it Leave it Love it Leave it Love it Leave it

Let him lay there, I wanted his headstone to read. What could I have been thinking. Even if his very words.

Where he is, in the utter absence of chlorophyll. How could he choose to be without trees.

We bought a string of bones from Bone Man that he cast a root curse on the developers; that they have a treeless afterlife. One endlessly paved forever.

If you have to go to traffic court, you can rent the boneman's staff, which he brought from his father's native Haiti. It makes an impression in the courtroom.

Even the Copilia, a mere speck, perceives images.

Her fallen porches. Her nonepitaph. Her other house invisible to strangers. Her manuscripts in the hands of warring kin.

When in Rome. Do as they done in Milledgeville. Once a bird sanctuary. That's right.

It is unlike night.

I wish I could see her now in all her incumbent glory. Tearing through the clouds in a chariot pulled by albino peahens.

You missed your turn. I said Pulltight Road. Where she lives with her dogs and her beautiful preemie baby and her wild iconographic creations.

Pulltight. I said.

My hands have changed. The fingers limber and lengthen.

The Eye Bank has more stock after Independence Day. Why don't you call back after the 4th.

Bear me along your light-bearing paths.

No more boiled peanuts for me. There's that smalltown swerve again. Pass with care.

I don't want to dream the boneman sticking thorns in my arm.
In that godless oven of a shed he calls an office. A bug got on me
in there I didn't recognize.

This oppressive little college has 23,000 acres. And that was
a wild turkey running across the campus. When we stop in
Admissions and ask for a catalog, we have to fill out a form,
and they indicate they will mail us one. Mutual paranoia floods
the senses.

Let's blow. I dare you to go in the bathroom in the student
union with this neon magic marker and write: Bite me you
big-balled boogie man.

Scatters Pool Hall. Let's go to a filling station and put on long
pants. Have ourselves an Icehouse.

It is unlike night.

He wanted to learn to play the piano by sitting on the brailled
score. It makes sense; playing with one hand, brailling with the
other is pretty inconvenient.

Just the sentence is chilling. I am a painter. I was a painter. I
once was a painter. And now I see. Not. The comfort of her
mother's white piano. The sweating silver vase with sunflowers.

Sunflower blindness.

Ghost hair nestled in streamers across the strings.

In the ceaselessly decomposing smoke of a pool hall. Seven green tables are racked under seven naked bulbs. The jukebox in the din calls the man a blanketyblankblank. If not the exact words the exact tenor. The plate glass casts glimpses of everything that has ever happened. The genesis of direction breaks and scatters.

The poor, miserable, garishly rich woman. Like fuchsia.
Wanting the reticence of crepe myrtle. Which is pitched higher
cr*e*pe or cr*a*pe. If I had them, they'd be in the backyard, they'd
be white. Immense, reticent, white bushes.

Hog Waste Lagoon is overflowing. *From the west down to*
the east.

Want an onion. They're Vidalias. Now do you know where
we are.

Did you ask the taxidermist about the eyes. Do you have to be
an ocularist as well. Was she the only woman in her class in
taxidermy school.

The ocularist has to build and design the eye, stain it; the iris
color, the veins and scleral tint must be perfect. Not a near
match. Only the wearer knows for sure.

Shit. I burned the shit out of my shit-eating tongue.

I said I had a mean streak. Whom do you meet in the mirror.

When we get to Paradise Garden let's call home. May the light
be optimal. Overcast. There is so much glass there.

God is Louise. Is that what it says.

I couldn't miss a mirror. I'd miss everything else. The whole chlorophylled sward.

Shelled butterbeans. The sign by itself makes me hungry. But who cooks beans in a motel. Unless one lived there.

The memory jug you bought. Did you hear a voice from within.

The name on the stone was Patience Fish. Isn't that nice. Near Cloud's Fly Shop.

The taxidermist. Did you say her name was Louise. Vomited the first three weeks.

They are strictly into columns. Our fingertips do not touch if we both stand here. Why it would take at least three long-armed men to encircle one. Ionic. Check the volutes.

The Roman who sold the memory jug

assured it were not stolen

from a grave. Near thrown

to the ground under the power.

At the moment of discovery.

The mouth of the jug remained

open and cool. As a well. A watery

sound emanated from within.

Though his sight were good then.

He were lost. Off Pulltight Road.

Ten years or more ago. The

sky, convict grey. Optimal.

For photographing. Responsive

to his surroundings. All matter

apprehended as one. Immanent.

Yet led there so separate.

Positioned parallel to and apart.

He parked the car. Shouldered

his tripod and walked around.

His last landscapes. Uninhibited

by temporality and men.

Because of the embedded bifocals,

baby spoon, mirror shards…

The jug shone on him.

Shewed itself. Chose him.

By the same gift of clarity

he owned the first wristwatch

in Rome, Georgia.

Thrasher said he had to share with us what was written on the bathroom wall: Bite me you big-balled boogie man. Maybe he meant b-a-l-d.

Like the man who made whirligigs who said his daddy taught him to shoot rabbits in the rocks. Maybe he meant actual rocks.

Why would anyone choose the absence of chlorophyll. Is orange really your favorite color. Don't you just love a trumpet vine.

And if thy left eye offend thee pluck it out.

I don't know about a chicken, but a cat will eat a cast-off eye. Chicken love. Cat eyes (come shining).

Morning glories. What's yours.

A chicken will eat anything. I have heard they stack the crates eight-high, and feed only the birds on top. A fact is a fact. Lore is lore. And drunk is drunk.

At present the white elephant is extinct. That's right, she said, they might come back. O go on.

O the chicken on the bottom. He would moan when we tailgated a Tyson truck.

He did not go see his brother in the hospital. He was ashamed of his lesions.

What's that spot on the wall. His brother said at last. That's god's hand said his mother who could not see the spot. Coming to take you home.

God is Louise.

Moss flew to the clotheslines on Ann Street on silver operatic wings.

His father took off work for two weeks. Without pay of course. And slept in the hospital bed with his 32-year-old son. Dad, I love you a bushel and a peck and a hug around the neck. That's child's talk. The father, 61, said.

Tears sheeting his cheeks. That's tenderness.

Do you like lamb germs, he asked his father. Lamb germs? I guess so son. I never thought about them before.

What's that spot on the wall.

Everybody in their bed needs love. Body love. Bible love. Blood love.

"Never avert your eyes." (Kurosawa)

"By the rays of Light I understand its least parts, and those as well successive in the same lines as contemporary in several lines." Tell it (Sir Isaac).

There. That saucer of light.

That's god's light son.

If I were born long long ago would you give me a zoetrope. It would be a most beloved toy.

He would take the doorknob into his study with him.

Don't touch that dial.

Long ago they called it a bleeding heart. She said from her porch. When I asked. Hers grew as tall as the lamppost. They call it something else nowadays.

Hannah she calls the sun.

Love it Leave it Love it Leave it Love it Leave it Love it Leave it Lo

Just stay quiet. Listen awhile. The white piano misses us. The white dog dreaming under the white bench is catching up with the cottontail.

The Mexicans say, not the man in the moon, but the rabbit strumming his *guitara*. Wonder what they say in Seoul. Or in Poetry.

When you go to pee, shut your eyes and grab a tree.

In the living room of a saint. Watching television. With an ice-cream headache. Assume lotus position. A documentary in black and white. Of young men and women with AIDS. Preparing to die. Communicating, wanting above all to be able to communicate, the alpha and omega of all things unfamiliar to us: Visions ringed with seas. The hatching of supernovae. Deep music. Balanced between two tones. July by lotuslight. Poetry at a standstill.

Trusting in the Haptic Sense

This has to be a watermelon.

This my hand, this yours.

This the heel of a foot. Nay, a potato, it's a potato, Baby.

That's a shovel.

That's a dress shoe.

The radio. The King James. Roses

they're not real though.

This is my number one guitar.

I bought it in downtown Macon in 19 and 42.

These are your prize peahens, I know them. Where's
    Becky at.

Between the *a* and the *t*.

Chicken hearts are good for the eyes. Full of zinc.

Mmmhmm.

Vitamin A help your retinas adjust.

Carrots and tomatoes are good, spinach, sweet potatoes,
    pumpkin.

Mmmhmm. Come sit alongside me

on this plasticky couch.

Let me put my arm up here.

Let me rove over to my good side now.

Let me see how large you are.

Let me squeeze your upper knee.

Let me inspect this velvety damp stuff. Unhuh.

Come my sultry refulgence,

can you name the four areas of surrender.
I do believe I smell
a rooster cooking. Mmmhmm.
That's how I know my young feeling has been restored
      to me.

Listen to that blind man say he smell a rooster cooking.

Pattycake lives here. She's one of the Jumping Foxes, the Double-Dutch Champs. Can you take her picture while we're here. I'll look for the funeral of a stranger to attend.

He's not rambling is he.

The end of the silver queen. I've got to have me one more cob before I croak.

Odontokeratoprosthesis: a tooth for an eye. A gruesome procedure, but not a bad trade.

The donor of course must not have syphilis. Why don't you call back after the 4th.

At one time Milledgeville was a bird sanctuary.

The worst is not so long as we can say, "This is the worst." Isn't that the truth. Deepstep now baby deepstep. Bear me along your light-bearing paths. Come shining.

I'm not long on ruins, but I wanted to stop. The walls of the church were intact. The chairs and pews were wrecked. But the baptismal font, with seven descending steps, I had never seen one emptied out. Trumpet vine in profusion over every brick and windowpane.

Mystery, mystery and a curse.

The watery grave. Take the boneman's hand.

Is that your cane slashing through the grass.

Deepstep come shining.

If I shell those beans for you, will you cook a mess for me. There goes Hannah behind that cloudlet.

>They hung in there when I was broke and sorry.
>They hung in there when I was mean and nasty.
>They hung in there when I was drunk and strung out.
>They hung on in.

After the iridectomy
the slow recognition of forms

A shirt on the floor looked like
the mouth of a well

Spots on a horse
horrible holes in its side

The sun in the tree
green hill of crystals

Moon over Milledgeville
only a story

Saucer of light on the wall
the hand of god

Especially in this town. Everybody needs love. House love. Dishes love. Moth-on-the-screendoor love, spot-on-the-wall love. That's god's hand. Known as the persistence of vision, the eyes' ability to perceive a series of still images as continuous motion.

Don't those totems scare you, Thrasher.

Hell, nothing scares me but real life. Bite me you big-balled boogie man.

What do you call those snakes with legs you make. I call them river dogs. I get the wood off the river. So I call them river dogs.

Ghosts have hair you know. It flies in on silver operatic wings.

I hope he has not mutilated himself. Maybe he meant b-a-l-d.

She had painted her trailer skirt to read: COMING SOON Jesus Christ in All His Glory. It's her trailer skirt, she can say what she likes. What she feels. What she believes. What she sees (Coming Soon).

Paint what you see. Undifferentiated dark. It is unlike night.

In the kingdom of cling peaches, fireworks, red ants.

Odontokeratoprosthesis. Literally a tooth for an eye. A
gruesome procedure. I won't go into it. But when the painter
went to Barcelona for the operation the surgeon took the sutures
out of his lids and said, Too late. You will never see.

The lids sewn shut like pockets on a new jacket. You must smell
your way to Dover.

The ruin under the lids. Voices emanating from the emptiness.
The memory jug's ancestors.

I am sorry. I mean for no one to come to such harm. But
vulnerability in a man. I find it very appealing. Forgive me. I do
not mean to intrude. Whereas cowardice is commonplace.
Among men. Vulnerability it's a rarity.

Early every evening she sits on the steps of her trailer. The dirt yard raked. Caterpillar fording the furrows. Mercy, Louise. If it wasn't hot hot hot. Cornlight. Eyes drink the color and are refreshed. Images seen but not interpreted. Thanks to her lovely twin trees the water she drew was cool. Cool the water she drank from the pump.

Stop at Bulldog's will you for a six-pack of Icehouse.

The cornea does the work. The back wall is the retina.

Just a drop of silver nitrate in the newborn's eyes. It's the law. In
case of syphilis. Thus are we treated as thieves in a department
store and syphilitics in a hospital. Even the newborn gets *the
treatment.*

We live by the etcetera principle.

All the cool people liked the children's humping line dance. All
the rest were horrified.

When in Rome...

By the rays of Light I understand its least parts, how my life
does not appear in cursive, but in handwrit letters. Crudely
executed.

SALVATION. DON'T LEAVE EARTH WITHOUT IT.

Ma'am, are these your glasses.

Here we live and breathe in all the glory of this Vidalia onion.
Lengths of pecan trees whipping by. Coming soon. In all his
glory. Suddenly I have the feeling of a great victory. A delirious
brilliance. Onionlight.

Corner of Hamlet and Bridges. A Jazz Messiah was born here 9/23/26. That's one little step for a man. Seven or eight Giant Steps for mankind. Empty, plate-glass light of Hamlet, North Carolina.

The door locked and the blue room opens only for private parties.

Don't touch that dial.

In the town with the clothesline ordinance the women are bleaching their teeth.

She has Casa Blanca lilies. I covet.

The fiddle contest will take place rain or shine.

Private-party love. By one sixty-watt bulb. And it be blue. The cool produces an halation. The couple standing underneath stir the floor as one. Some modeling on the side of the face. When directly below the bulb. All other detail dropped out. The eye gradually grows accustomed to this. The music circling. Huge and dark. *Eroico furore.* Supremely insane. Accelerated arpeggios. Unchain a cruel streak. Breath. Nerve. Mind. Pain. Teeming tonal centres. D-state. Nocturnal emission of sperm. Corner of Hamlet and Bridges. And in the last year. They say he did. See angels. A synergism of cancer and dwelling in musical extremis.

Get the hell out of here. Can't you see I'm not dressed. Can't you see. Anything.

If it's too hot or too cold or there's too much nitrogen in the dirt tomatoes won't set. How can I look my old daddy in the face and say I can no longer bring a tomato to set.

Lights out, Hon.

During which, the hatching of supernovae. Acres and acres of them.

Corner of Hamlet and Bridges. Did you say he met a woman there that went by Louise?

My hands have changed. Deepstep baby. It's zero visibility. And the fish aren't biting.

I left my chicory-blue swimsuit in Augusta. Where you left the grey hair diffuser. When you asked your mother when her red hair began to grey. She looked at you like you were crazy, How the hell should I know. The first few she plucked; thereafter, her purses were never without foils of henna.

The light is antebellum. Ionian man. Everybody inhale.

I had an operation on my back, between my shoulder blades. A potato-sized stone was set in. I recognize the ones who have had this operation.

No. Pattycake was Pie's husband. He brought her a sack of robins.

Look-alikes fall in love.

My family loves cream corn.

Her scarves were made from the whiskers of wild Himalayan goats. He fell into her sensorium. There was nothing left for me to do but fold.

If I offer a breakfast of peasant bread and milk. If I practice the poetry of secession. If I tell you my words are not feathered.

I left my chicory-blue swimsuit back at the motel where the baseball team cannonballed us out of the pool. They won the first day because they played smart ball. The next day they lost because they stayed up all night and didn't play smart ball. When asked his position, the bucktooth said he rode the pines.

Some ghost hair flew into the room and collapsed over the lampshade.

He was willing to let the paintings he destroyed stand for him. His despair absented him from the chlorophylled world.

Weird planets of the eyeballs orbiting the abyss.

He feels only a certain tightness about the eyes.

Push his nose. He'll let you off on whatever floor you want.

God bless the Lumière brothers. Lead us, guide us. We are crossing over one by one.

Did you see that. Sorry. It was one of those followers of what's-his-face that throw birds in cars at stoplights.

I don't like B&Bs. I don't like to talk to the host. Let's go to an Indian-owned-and-operated place. A Jenny Lind Motel. Pay up and shut up. Cable, a/c, pool, and no bedbugs.

Don't park in the shade on my account.

OK. One B&B. Colonel Yancy's. The young, urban, African-American professional in the Colonel's eyelet-canopied bed, sent down from Charlotte to set up a branch bank. Why do you think he had a vault in his hall. He didn't trust banks. Forget female African-American bankers. Take a deepstep, Colonel. Your time is done gone.

Love it Leave it Love it Leave it Love it Leave it Love it
Love it Lea

The donor of course must not have syphilis.

Doctor S.L. Bigger, captured by the Bedouins, kept a pet antelope, blind in one eye. He took out a fresh-killed antelope's eye, and put it in his pet's head, and the pet saw whole again.

My tomatoes are as tall as this post. And nary a tomato on them. Do you think I am under a curse.

He's not out rambling is he.

She wanted to buy the stuffed bobcat in the antique store, but the owner said it was his logo.

A wild turkey running across the road right on the campus. 23,000 acres. A kingdom. I wouldn't go to school there for love or money.

And if thy right eye offend thee pluck it out.

Cold eyes are bad to eat.

These gourds are kindly expensive. But would you wont anythang that wasn't.

I see your point.

As a child I was a kleptomaniac. But I'm a very nice person now. I wouldn't take a napkin without my doctor's permission.

When the lightning hit the mute swan. In all her glory. The students were traumatized. They were in the refectory overlooking the lake. When the lightning hit the mute swan. In all her glory. She exploded. Her five cygnets sizzled on the surface.

There will be no more night.

When I lay my hand on the live oak I wondered how many pencils would it yield. Pencils of days and of hips and lilies. Pencils of Novocain and commotion.

That self-conscious Southern poetry, preposterous as a wedding dress.

The old washing machine Clyde uses to make her papier-mâché from the *Atlanta Constitution*. Finally broke. She'll never find parts.

```
          W     E
        A   EU  P L
ST          O
  T P       E       L
        H   O       L
  T P H     E             S
                         TS
              F P L T
  S     H     E
        HRA EU            D
        H     E   R
          H A       PB    D
            O             T
  TK          E     P
        HR  EU
  T P       U R
            O             D
        PW  A     R B G
                  R B G S
  TKPW R O        P   G
  T P   O         R       T
        A         R
            E
        A
              F
  TK      A     R B G
          E             S
    K       O       L
            O     R
              F P L T
  T
  T       R   U   PB G S
      W   O       B
    P   A   EU  PB  T
                        D
      W A
    P   A         L
            E           T
              F P L T
  S         O     L
      W   O   EU        DS
  TK        E
  S     R   E     L
            O     P
  T P R                 T
  S         E   PB
  T         E   R
            O U         T
      W A       R    DS
              F P L T
          A
  S     R O EU          D
                        G
  T P H   EU
    K       EU  PB      D
              F
        HR  EU  PB
              F P L T
  T
    PW  O               D
            EU
```

When the aim is to feel wholeness itself. She laid her hand on the deeply furrowed bark, groping for the area of darkest color. The trunks would be painted with a palette. Solids would develop from the center outward. Avoiding any kind of line. The body pressed against the trunk until she were certain of being extinguished by the darkness. One achieves a concealed drawing. Which is most like night.

The Colonel's curtains whiten in unelaborating rays. His clawfoot tubs. Big-tub love.

What's that spot on the wall. That light saucer.

She wanted to fall to her knees under petals of snow. In a stark white dormitory. Twelve white cakes would be brought to a cloth-draped table by twelve starched women. All of this mystery, mystery, mystery.

If I can't coax a twelve-foot tomato plant to yield one juicy mouthful. I must be under a curse.

What if we stay here long enough to attend a stranger's funeral. I like this spot.

And when the sudarium was removed, wrap by wrap...
Too late the doctor said. You will never see.

Look-alikes fall in love. Unless...

O my irises. My irises. O the sidewalls of my breasts.

It reminds me of my back life. If I had stayed I would have married the no-count. He couldn't help it. He had no luck. They took his luck and tied it to a rabbit's neck.

Trailer living was appealing when I was seventeen.

We need a preponderance of love.

Ride. Eat. Sleep. It said on his T-shirt.

The darkness will eat you. They say in Bosnia.

The LED emits the following diode: This is the time to see and to feel WHOLES.

Color. Degree of brightness. Saturation: Hue. Value. Chroma. He had a passion for nomenclature.

Ride. Eat. Sleep

Oncet   after a heavy rain

he come back   at daybreak

threw down a few dollars and cents

alongside a set   of pretty glass eyes

into a little dish on the dresser

flopped crosswise on the bed and slept

I started to write   I feel lost here

and I'm going to go home   Oncet

I clave to him   like fog but the bus

at Dahlonega   wasn't waiting for me

to go through the old lucubrations

and Brother Veal of Deepstep nor was I

Could I have a touch of your vitreous humor.

What does she look like, the handsome young blind man asked his pretty, freckled girl at the festival.

She has black hair. Strange, he said. I pictured her blond.

The rain would let up and then it would start up. Some brought umbrellas. Some turned garbage bags into ponchos.

The refrain to the rain would be a movement up and down the clefs of light.

The boats in the bay took in the festival from the water.

Blur in. Blur out.

The darkness will eat you.

A bullet don't have nobody's name on it.

HAIR TODAY. GONE TOMORROW. (sign at the electrolysis center) Dontouchmymustache. That's all the Japanese I can say.

They didn't have a metal detector. So you know folks were packing. Club Paradise. Saturday night. Bowlegs Miller led the house band.

What are you going to do when our lamps are gone out.

What are you going to do.

What are you going to do when you come to the crossroad.

Everybody in this clinic needs love. A preponderance of love.

The eye is an image-catching device. On this much we are agreed.

They dropped silver nitrate in my new baby's eyes. According to law. A poisonous colorless crystalline compound. Used in manufacturing photographic film, silvering mirrors, dyeing hair, plating silver, and in medicine as a cautery and antiseptic.

```
ST P H        F P L T
ST P H        F P L T
   T P      EU R    S
                     T
      HR   EU        T
   S       EU  PB G S
   T     O
   S   H A             D
         O            S
              F P L T
   T
   S   H A             D
         O            S
      PW           B G
   T P HRAO            D
                      D

      W
      PW R O          D
      W A     R B
                     S
              F
   TK    A    R B G
              F P L T
      W A     R B
              F P L T
         A           S
                     T
   TK    A    R B G
    K      O    P L S
              E  PB
   T       EU R
      HR   EU
   T P H
   T       O       TS
           O   PB
              F P L T
      W A     R B
              F P L T
   T
      HR  EU       T
                B G
              E       T
              E  PB
              F P L T
   TK         E
   S    R O  U R      D
              F R L T
   S    A
   T P H O    R
              U       S
   S          E R     T
              EU
              F       T
   TK    A    R B G
              F P L T
      W A
   S          E      TS
                     T
```

First the light sinks to shadows. The shadows become
flooded with broad washes of dark. Watch. As the dark comes
entirely into its own. Watch. The light being eaten. Devoured.
Sonorous certainty of the dark. What sets the hangers in a
closet singing in unison. The light murdered, that the truth
become apparent.

Is that why the newborn looks like an alien. Or did the grey
ones inseminate me. Do the grey ones know I am not a proper
specimen.

God is Louise. Louise moves in mysterious ways. Coming soon.

Are we not fearfully and wonderfully made.

Tell those Lumière brothers, I appreciate everthang they done.

If I tell you it's a ten-dollar bill how are you going to know the
difference if it's a one. If I tell the house painter, eggshell white,
how do I know she won't paint it orange. Trumpet-flower orange.

Ride. Eat. Sleep. Where on earth will we go next. What will we
do when the money is gone. What're you going to do when your
lamp's gone down. Tuck your shirttail in.

Word spreads.

The first menses in the dark days, winter. Born blind, early onset.

Lead me to the river with your mirror.
Unwrap the sudarium from my face.
Lead me, guide me, to the faraway deep down. Then steal away
in alligatorlight.

Which is brighter g-r-a-y or g-r-e-y. Which is pitched higher.

How do I look. I have forgotten. Deepstep come shining.

For I am the cipher in her story in which she robbed his grave
of its voice and appears herself as an old angel. All that is there is
the ghost of his breath. The hair of his ghost got caught up in
my lines. In the night it flew here. It is the hair that makes it
so mysterious.

O your giant TV. Do you watch much. What is there to watch.
This is the time to see and to feel WHOLES.

Blur in. Blur out.

Were we not fearfully and wonderfully made.

I always did have a spidery hand. You know what it says.

Is this the hand that will lead me to the river. Lead me along
your light-bearing paths. Do you leave the mirror in the river.

We were young. We was happy. Were we not. Happy. Young.
Wasn't we.

The eye is a mere mechanical instrument.

Leaning over the white piano, breathing in her petals. The mute
swan exploded. With the students looking on. In all her glory.

A white house among the white hydrangea trees.

Now that is an Arkansas toe sticking out from that sheet if I ever saw one.

She wears me out. Doesn't she you. Can't she play anything else.

Is this where he swapped a motorcycle that didn't work for a pinball machine that didn't work.

It is not that we live in a world of colored objects but that surfaces reflect a certain portion of the light hitting them. It's all whiteness. Here, in Ultima Thule.

The noise of the retina as you get older.

Known by her neighbors to garden by flashlight. Sometimes, she said, the darkness creeps up on me.

Whenever I see a walk-ins-welcome sign I want to walk on in. Whenever I see a we-reserve-the-right-to-refuse-service-to-anyone sign I want to shake my white panties at the boss.

Suddenly I have the feeling of a great victory.

Then there's the no-shoe-no-shirt-no-service; the you-break-it-you-pay-for-it. And the employees-must-pluck-out-an-eye-before-returning-to-work.

Blur in. Blur out. Just a hypothetical blind woman brought
out of completest dark. Looking at a face. She will know it
belongs to Pattycake if Pattycake laughs. Counting trees by
the shadow of their trunk. Looking at something blue. That's
the river. Something green. That's the grass. Something else
blue. That's sky. Stood mutely in front of a lone tree. Sees
only the spaces in between. That's the tree with the lights
in it. Tuck your shirttail in. Now this. Is my very own hand.
I always did have a spidery hand.

After he lost his sight, he could discriminate colors by their vibration. He was thrown to the ground under the power.

The water here, black marble. The grass, army-surplus green.

Poking around in the woods with a gun. Poke around in the house with a book. Poke around. Poke around.

They bleach their teeth those women.

Are those Casa Blanca lilies. I covet.

We lunch on Onion River. Stop by Cloud's Fly Shop.

Fiddle contest tomorrow rain or shine.

Get the hell out of here, can't you see I'm not dressed. Can't you see I'm depressed.

I see. I see.

Please don't put your feet on the chairs, it said in the eye doctor's office. Please don't spit on the floor, it said in my father's courtroom.

Her Aunt Flo said she hadn't had any in so long she'd done growed back together.

Are you still working on that drink.

Cold pop. Free sir. Sold here.

We never close. Every nickel counts. Just ask Big Sam. He suctioned every nickel from every small town pocket and he sewed it under his lids, a veritable sheik from Arkansas.

He put a pillow over her mother's head and shot her. The white piano shivered in the corner like a boy with an orchid.

That was a helluva note.

After the iridectomy
she fell to the ground under the power

The boxwoods that lined the road
were walking with her

She could touch the willow wands on the other side of Little
Lynches River

She smudged the passage she had once felt

She was fearful of putting a morsel of cake
in her mouth

She thought it too large to enter in

A pool of shade appeared bottomless

The contours of a man were horrible to her
those of the family dog were bearable

A pool of shade appeared bottomless

Two white horses side by side. Going to take her on her farewell ride.

Ain't it hawd.

Half-fare, blind, mmhmm.

Nothing in the world beats time.

She said her sister was more like Aunt Flo everyday. Big blond Aunt Flora with the smutty mouth who said she hadn't had any in so long it'd done growed back together.

In the gated communities the women are bleaching their teeth.

Shielding her eyes among her Casa Blanca lilies with a tad of a hangover she offers spiderweb to staunch his paper cut.

Cloud's Fly Shop in spitting distance.

Fiddle contest rain or shine, declares the flyer on the creosote pole.

I see. I see.

Don't you just hate it when your gown catches between your buttocks.

Don't you just hate it when the waiter says, Are you still working on that drink.

Poke around. Poke around. Can't you see I'm depressed.
Welcome to my sensorium. You can touch, but you cannot lie.

You must know the Veals of Deepstep.

Mother's neighbor passes on her mower, riding (*sic*) her Clancy novel.

She suffers from what Wittgenstein called aspect blindness. Is it a rabbit. Nay, it's a swan, a swan.

Branches drop without warning. Clouds accumulate around a kind of idea akin to sonic weight. Progressive darkness. 250 miles offshore with winds at 105 MPH, Bertha turns inland. Multitudes of windows crossed with masking tape. Evacuation mandatory in the low-lying areas. Contrasts annihilated. Concealing loneliness and fear. As when the lens opening is too small. Taken too late. Or too early. Uncharacteristic silence loading the car. Worry over maundering. Hunger over worry. Tranquilized with a private jukebox in Formicalight. Endless refills. Pigs-in-the-blanket-and-grits-on-the-side time. Beats the bejesus out of Bertha's maw. Now do you know where you are. My over-air-conditioned-and-caffeinated love.

Come shining. I have you in hand, Deepstep.

That's Junebug's place. It's a mess. He was way old a long time before I ever was born. His daddy was a Senator. Lived at Twelve Oaks. Tornado pulled up all twelve and tossed them in the fields like drinking straws. Without the oaks it looks like an asylum. For the criminally insane.

She was my friendgirl for three years. We were thick. Then she ran off and got married. Her mother and I sat on the scratchy plaid sofa crying. Too young. Too young.

> She hung on in when they runover his dog.
> She hung on in when he caught his hand in the trolling
>   motor.
> She hung on in when he starting talking out of his head.
> She hung on in when he flunked the polygraph.
> She hung on in.

Come on, Hon. If you come undone. I come undone. You take two eggs over or one.

Sixteen. The white piano shivered in the dark like a boy with an orchid.

He set fire to his birthday present, the white angora sweater, in the judge's driveway. Because she wouldn't go all the way.

I see, I see.

The Veals of Deepstep. They are very prominent.

Bright light flooded in horizontally from the left.

It fell obliquely on her body, which subtly responded to the interruption.

If Louise is god can her evanescence be fixed.

The amount of sunlight striking each one of her pearls.

Don't disabuse her, the grass widow of her aura of originality *with her pearls and her amphetamines.*

The scrape of chairs on a stone floor. A sack of birds escaped in the house. Fleshy, velvety dampness. Panic. Time lapse. Silence. That they think only of sight while they chew. Slowly the hand unwraps the bandages. Until the night shuts like a door. And the light slams from his face. Interrupting the flow of stimuli. It is all whiteness, he says, even this sightlessness.

Besides, even a rat can strike a match.

The politics are so deep. Ceaselessly, yes ceaselessly.

The moon is vagrant and the prey senses the predator's warm breath; the hale sleep naked atop the sheet.

How Walt's saintly white beard was reported to attract butterflies.

Her late husband was a poet. He had some beautiful thoughts. He published in *Ideal* and other places. He had all kinds of rhyme schemes and everything. So meticulous. Sometimes. It would make you think.

That's right. An ordinary rat can scratch a match, and burn a good house down to the ground.

Forms nearest the eye appeared blurred. We have been separated by a chair. The blind man taught my uncle to cane in an afternoon. He found the chair in Mamo's attic. It took him two weeks. And then his wife did the stenciling.

Gold leaf is obtainable in small booklets. But it'll cost you.

Stole a watermelon oncet. Stole some sugar.

Remember me to all of them. Bite everybody on the lips for me. Remember me forever.

Recuerda me siempre. It says on the blade of the knife he hung from a string. The tip of it twirling over his pillow while he dreamed. How that man loved to dream.

Salvation. Don't leave earth without it. Or your glasses. There is so much to see.

Pattycake was Pie's husband.

Caution. Deep step.

Photo graphein of an old plaid couch in a field as its sunken cushions emptied of bodies and filled with leaves, then snow, then rain; then the seams split and the batting bubbled out for the birds and squirrels to carry off by the beak- and clawful.

Don't touch that dial. Here's the rest of the story: These three ladies they had been into all manner of wrongdoing. They were wearing the evil one's varsity jacket. They were hot for god and they were on fire. That night they were thrown to the ground under the power. That night the glory cloud filled the church. The prayer line stayed open that night. A real hard light, sharp, cold as a nail, split right through the boards. Angels went to banging around in the rafters like barn swallows. We'll pick up at the next chapter, dearly beloveds...

He hogged the bed.
She hogged the covers.
He hogged the meat.
She hogged the conversation.

Hush, hogs, hush.

She hung on in. *With her pearls and her amphetamines.*

A pencil of rays was all that he could make out. He would be shewn the rest by touch.

Images may be either real or virtual.

Hearing is the last sense to go.

Did you ask Thrasher if that was a lapdog in his freezer.

I thought you were taking pictures of the Double-Dutch Champs.

The funeral was postponed until tomorrow.

Stay here with me. If you don't mind the dark. We can talk until the tape runs out. It has the aura of an original.

If Louise is the answer what is the question. Are we stuck here
or what. Anyway, the singing's not helping much.

Who's there. Is that you, Deep Step.

O my irises. My irises. And the sidewalls of my breasts.

See this hand. See this. Come shining.
The hand that peeled the bark from my birches.
The hand that stirred the pencil of my life.
That took a belt to my hebetude.
The hand that explored my body cavities, hand of the
        selenographer, mapper of lost roads.
That picked my bones (white).
The hand that anticipated everything. While the fishermen
        of Borneo were stealing telephone booths.
That took me in deep (step by step).
That prepared my colors.
Then picked my brain (clean).
The hand that pulled my last Vidalia out of the garden and
        ate it dirt, bulb, and green.
That spread itself out on my window.
Eidolon of light (even as it decomposes).
Then made known to me the deep blindness of coitus and
        denied me a ladder to see out.

We can't send this message   no positive way

hallelujah   glory to ya   they call it the hump

day   if you can get over the hump you've got it

made   position yourself to hear

somewhere around the 14th verse   we need

an elevator   to help us look in the present

to help us visualize the future   thank you

for your call   can't you see   not of this

world   who has no way   somebody say   what is

a leader   who knows the way   goes the way

shows the way   just in case

somebody doesn't know   what I'm talking

about   the commission to be a friend

to the lost people   this goes out to the air

the sweet barbecue of night   I want to

magnify   praise is the gate   to enter in

sit down   I said please sit down   the more

you praise the clearer the mind becomes   I said I

love you   I adore you   I called didn't I   praise is

the gate   to enter in   we need an elevator   to
take our lost friends up   to the auditorium
of light   didn't I call   O world world world
I but stumbled when I saw   praise is the gate
to enter   plenty of parking   come early
to get a good seat

Look for a clear object (Case #33)

Don't need a magnifying glass

To make the feelings seen

Softly unwrap bandages

Unlike paper torn off a wall

Place yourself inside the damage

Lights approaching top speed

Blur in, blur out

A need for linear relief

Everything going awful fast

Trees agitated by wind

Keep the setting simple

A bowl of sugar on a table

Separated by a chair

Not an inkling what it means

Urge to withdraw

Pull the ladder up after

```
      P   A          TS
              F P L    T
T P H                  T
      H     EU         T
            E   R
      W   O     R L   D
            EU
          O   FR
      A
      W   O     PB    S
      AO  EU
                PB
      AO  EU
T P   O     R
      AO  EU
          A         L
T   H   EU
                  R B G S
          O
      P   A         B G
      A           PB


      R   E F
          E
      HRA
T         O    R
          EU
                R B G S
S             E        S
      HR    E          S
      HR    EU
      PW       U RPB G
              F P L T
T P H   EU
      W   O     PB
      H   O            S
              FR B
T   HR    U
          A
T P       EU R
T P H O             S
      H O   U
TK        E F


ST    A          T
                 G
  T
  K               B
              F P L T
T
T P        U RPB
T          U R
      HR O            S
                R B G S
      PW AO        B G S
K  HR   E       B G D
          O   FR
T   H   EU R     T
          EU
KWR     E     S
```

In the hither world I lead you willingly along the light-bearing paths. In the hither world I offer a once-and-for-all thing, opaque and revelatory, ceaselessly burning. Anyone who has ever been through a fire knows how devastating it can be. The furniture lost, books collected over thirty years, the mother's white piano. I was there. I know.

Stimulants, Poultices, Goads

Opticks or a Treatise of the Reflections, Refractions, Inflections and Colours of Light by Sir Isaac Newton; Forrest Gander, Akira Kurosawa, *Smoke,* Bone Man, Snake Man, Norman Schwarzkopf, James Agee, *Georgia: The WPA Guide to Its Towns and Countryside, Farmer's Almanac*; WBY, the Beatles, James Dickey, Frank Stanford, Holy Bible; *The Book of Common Prayer*; *Eclipse: A Nightmare* by Hughes DeMontalembert; Bob Dylan, Flannery O'Connor, Roger Dorset, the Lumière brothers, Margaret Vittitow, Carolyn Merritt, John Coltrane, Peter Gurnis, Shelby Morgan, Deborah Luster, *Encyclopædia Britannica*; Paradise Garden, Stephen Beard, Stephen Engstrom, Bill Smart, Matthew 5:27–30, *King Lear*; *The Art of Cézanne* by Kurt Badt; *Blake* by Peter Ackroyd; *It Came from Memphis* by Robert Gordon; Aunt Mildred, Paul Harvey, *A Pair of Blue Eyes* by Thomas Hardy; Ft. Lauderdale radio ministry; Vic Chesnutt's *Is the Actor Happy*; *Vision and Design* by Roger Fry; *Space and Sight* by M. von Seden; *Howard Finster: Man of Visions* by J.F. Turner; station WLLL; *The Freedom Principle: Jazz after 1958* by John Litweiler; Reverend Pearly Brown, Anne Truitt, *Mental Healers* by Stefan Zweig; Alyce Collins Wright, court reporter (retired); Virginia Center for the Creative Arts and its artist fellows in the summer of 1996.

About the Author

C.D. Wright has published eight collections of poetry, most recently *Tremble* (Ecco Press, 1996), and *Just Whistle,* a booklength poem in collaboration with the photographer Deborah Luster (Kelsey Street Press, 1993). Wright's awards include the Poetry Center Book Award, the Witter Bynner Prize from the American Academy and Institute of Arts and Letters, a General Electric Award for the literary essay, a Whiting, and a Rhode Island Governor's Award for the Arts. In 1981 she received a Fellowship from the National Endowment for the Arts, which prompted a move to Mexico, and in 1987 Fellowships from the Guggenheim Foundation and the Bunting Institute. A second NEA was awarded in 1988. In 1994 she was named State Poet of Rhode Island, a five-year post. On a fellowship for writers from the Lila Wallace–Reader's Digest Foundation, Wright curated "a walk-in book of Arkansas" multimedia exhibition that toured throughout her native state for a two-year period. Wright teaches at Brown University. With poet Forrest Gander she edits Lost Roads Publishers. They live with their son Brecht near Providence, Rhode Island.

lmer, originally cut by
Baskerville and Caslon,
of the "modern" style
tury. Design and com-
sign by John D. Berry.
latfelter Author's Text
nting.